J. D Breen

Anglican Orders - Are they Valid?

A Letter to a Friend

J. D Breen

Anglican Orders - Are they Valid?
A Letter to a Friend

ISBN/EAN: 9783337107406

Printed in Europe, USA, Canada, Australia, Japan

Cover: Foto ©Lupo / pixelio.de

More available books at **www.hansebooks.com**

ANGLICAN ORDERS:

ARE THEY VALID?

A Letter to a Friend.

BY

J. D. BREEN, O.S.B.

"Ergo inimicus vobis factus sum, verum dicens vobis?"—
Gal. iv. 16.

LONDON:

BURNS, OATES & CO.,

17 & 18, PORTMAN STREET, & 63, PATERNOSTER ROW.

1877.

PREFACE.

THE following pages were not originally intended for the press.

They were written to furnish a friend, who was unable to examine the question for himself in more elaborate works, with an answer to the query in the title-page, and to place before him, in a plain and simple way, the chief reasons why that answer must be given. It was thought by some, to whose opinion deference was due, that they would be useful to others who were in the same position as the person to whom they were in the first instance addressed, and at their suggestion they are now given to the public.

I may mention that the extracts from Harding quoted at p. 31 may be found in the Parker Society's edition of Jewel's works, vol. iii. pp. 320-1, 334, &c.; and that respecting the Council of Trent, quoted p. 34, in Waterworth's work on the subject.

The statement (p. 41) regarding the baptism of some Protestant bishops receives considerable support from Dr. Lee's "Life of Rev. R. S. Hawker." In the Appendix to that work are given the reasons for supposing that Dr. Tait, the present possessor of the see of Canterbury, has not had valid Christian baptism. Very grave reasons they are, though they do not apply to his case alone.

J. D. B.

CHELTENHAM, *Feb.* 22, 1877.

ANGLICAN ORDERS:

ARE THEY VALID?

I HAVE received a letter from you, in which you set before me the difficulties in matters of religion that perplex you, and ask my advice in the *doubts* that harass your soul. I accept with pleasure the confidence you are pleased to repose in me, and I trust you will never have any reason to regret that you have done so. You may rest assured that my best advice is always and at all times at your service, and that any question you think fit to raise shall receive my most serious consideration.

Your communication has given me great pleasure, also, on other grounds : (1) because it shows that you are thinking, and that the grace of God is stirring within you ; and (2) because of your expressed resolve to allow no earthly consideration to hinder you from following the Divine call, and becoming an obedient child of the Church of God, once your intellect is satisfied where that Church is to be found. This resolve is worthy of you, and cannot fail to obtain the blessing it deserves, both of light and grace. At all events, it is more than

B

sufficient to engage in your regard the sympathies of any one who has the heart of the *"Bonus animarum Pastor."* It is not the fact that you differ from me that can ever separate us. This has arisen from accidents of birth and education, which we may regret, but over which we have had no control, and can furnish no ground of itself for not extending to you that "peace on earth towards men of *good-will*" which our Lord wished to be the inheritance of all those who truly sought Him. It is this *good-will* in you, your love of God, and your desire to do His holy Will at all costs, that unites us in spirit more than any external circumstance can part us in body; and makes me long for the day when we, who are already so joined together in heart and desire, may no longer be separated in outward communion.

This is the spirit in which I have learned from St. Augustine that those from without are to be approached, if we would have our words receive that attention which we may think they deserve.

"Let those," he says, "treat you harshly who are not acquainted with the difficulty of attaining to truth and avoiding error. Let those treat you harshly who know not how hard it is to get rid of old prejudices. Let those treat you harshly who have not learned how very hard it is to purify the interior eye, and render it capable of contemplating the sun of the soul—truth. But as for us, we are far from this disposition towards persons who are separated from us, not by errors of their own invention, but by being entangled in those of others. We are so far from this disposition that we pray to God that, in refuting the false opinions of those whom you follow, not from malice, but imprudence, He would bestow upon us that spirit of peace which feels no other sentiment than charity; and has no other interest than that of Jesus Christ, no other wish but for your salvation." (Contra Ep. Fund., i, c. ii.)

You tell me that, as far as your information goes, you see no reason to doubt the validity of Anglican orders, and that this is to you a point of such importance that it justifies, if it does not compel, your continuing a member of the Church of your baptism.

You have, you say, the Apostolic Succession, the Priesthood, the Real Presence of our Lord in the Blessed Sacrament ; and what more can any one desire ?

I am far from agreeing with you that the question of the validity of your orders occupies a place of such primary importance as you seem to suppose. It is, of course, true that valid orders must necessarily be found in the true Church of Christ, for they are necessary to her supernatural life, and, in fact, to her very existence ; still, it does not by any means follow, that valid orders are a *note* of the true Church, and that those who possess them are necessarily within the One Fold of the One Shepherd. Nothing could be further from the truth. Any such inference is a logical fallacy.

There are, unfortunately, many men going about the world who have received the imposition of hands, whose souls have been stamped with that character of the priesthood which eternity itself is powerless to efface, and yet whose lives are a wreck, and whose office is a failure. They are unfortunate priests who, in their fall, can be compared only to Lucifer. It may be that they are apostates, it may be they are reprobates—let them have fallen as they may, still they are priests, still they are ordered verily and indeed ; and yet they may have no more claim to be considered, formally, children

of the Church of God than the veriest Pagan that
ever lived.

What is true of individuals is true also of religious bodies. At no period in the history of the
Church have valid orders been accepted as evidence
that the parties who possessed them had not suffered
shipwreck concerning the faith. Most of the great
heresies of the early ages were in possession of
orders of unquestionable validity ; nevertheless, in
deciding whether their following were to be cut off
from the communion of the Church as obstinate
heretics or not, this was a point which was allowed
to have no weight whatsoever.

In fact, I can at present recall very few instances
of a religious body of any consequence which has
revolted against the See of Peter—besides the
Anglican Establishment—whose orders have been
disallowed by the Church. Your argument, therefore, We belong to the true Church because we
have valid orders, will not stand.

Not only is the possession of valid orders quite
inadequate, of itself, to establish your claim to be
within the fold of the Church, but it is extremely
doubtful whether such an inheritance at all im-
proves the condition of those who are in other
respects *extra Ecclesiam*—whether it is not an
aggravation of the guilt of schism, or, at any rate,
a sort of white elephant, a gift which it is difficult
to know what to do with, and which it is better to
be without.

The dangers of sacrilege that encompass such
persons are innumerable. There can be no doubt
that to rend the seamless garment of Christ by
schism or heresy is one of the deadliest sins which
it is in the power of man to commit, and that those
who approach the sacraments with any such stain
upon their souls, trample under foot the Blood of

our Lord. Now, in order that those who are entangled in schism or heresy may come to the altar with clean hands, it is necessary that their good faith be so perfect as entirely to free them from all responsibility, or complicity, not only with those who do such things, but also with those who consent to or communicate with those who do them.

This is no light matter. The number of souls is easily counted who, by reason of their neglect of prayer, carelessness about sin, worldliness, and religious indifference, are not to some extent answerable to God for being what they are.

There is, moreover, such a thing as receiving valid sacraments fruitlessly, by reason of some impediment existing in the soul, which hinders them from producing their proper effect, the grace of God. On the part of the recipient certain dispositions are required as necessary conditions to prepare the soul for the operations of Divine grace, and this preparation must commence by removing the obstacles that would hinder its working. Fire, for instance, will not melt the flinty rock, nor consume green wood, and the nullity of result is due, not to any impotence on the part of the agent, but to the unsuitable nature of the substance with which it is brought in contact. So with the soul of man. "He that *believeth* and is baptized shall be saved. He that believeth not shall be condemned" (Mark xvi. 16).

This valid, though fruitless, reception of a sacrament may very easily occur in the case of the Blessed Sacrament. A person may approach Holy Communion in the most perfect good faith, who has confessed his sins with attrition only to a priest who has no jurisdiction whatsoever to absolve him, and whose absolution is therefore null and void. In the case of an Anglican clergyman—the question of orders apart—the only source from which he could profess to derive his spiritual jurisdiction would be from a Bishop, who holds his jurisdiction from the Crown ; and yet he has not even a colourable pretext for claiming to act in virtue of any such commission when hearing confessions, for he would, as a rule, have to act in defiance of, rather than in obedience to, the authority of his Bishop, if he attempted to do so.

Putting aside for a moment the question of validity, all such absolutions would be invalid on the score of want of jurisdiction, and the party who in good faith might approach the altar on the strength of having received such an absolution only with attrition, would not indeed commit a formal sacrilege, but still would not receive the benefit of the Sacrament, because he has sin upon his soul, and its presence there is a bar to the entrance of the Holy Spirit under his roof.   The most that we can positively assert is, that such a one has saved himself from the guilt of receiving unworthily ; for whether God will supply, by the working of His unfettered Spirit, in reward for his good will, what has not come to him through the ordinary channel, is a mystery, which can only be known on that day when the secrets of all hearts shall be revealed.

This clear conscience in dealing with holy things can only be true of those who are in the most perfect good faith, and upon whose souls has not rested any serious shadow of a doubt.

So that the fact of your having fruitful sacraments in the case of adults not in danger of death depends more on your being in the Church than having real orders.

St. Augustine (Contra Litteras Petiliani, lib. iii. c. 1)* writes thus, as to the effect which schism

* Gaume, iii. page 503.

has in impeding the fruit of the sacraments:—" For if the baptism which Pretextatus and Felicianus have administered in the communion of Maximianus was theirs, why has it been acknowledged by you in those whom they baptized, as if it were Christ's? But if it is Christ's—as it truly is—it could be of no avail to those who had received it with the crime of schism. Of what avail do you say it could be to those whom you have received with the same baptism, except that—after the crime of their wicked separation had been blotted out by the bond of peace—they would not be obliged to receive the sacrament of holy baptism, as if they had it not; but that, as what they possessed before was to their hurt, so now it might begin to be to their advantage? But if this has not been furnished them in your communion—because it cannot be furnished to schismatics among schismatics—it is, however, supplied to you in the Catholic communion ; not that you receive baptism as if it were wanting in you, but that that which you have received becomes fruitful. For all the sacraments of Christ are received, not to our salvation, but to our condemnation, when without the charity of the unity of Christ."

Again,* he says, in his discourse to the people of the Church of Cæsarea, "Outside the Catholic Church, he " [the schismatical bishop] " can have everything except salvation. He can have honour, he can have the sacrament, he can sing Alleluia, he can answer Amen, he can believe the Gospel, he can both have and preach the faith ; but nowhere, except in the Catholic Church, can he find salvation."

Again,† "So when any of the Donatists come over to us, we accept not their faults; to wit, their dissen-

---

* Gaume, ix. page 947.   † Gaume, ii. page 222.

sion and error, which are rejected as hindrances to concord ; and then we embrace them as brethren, standing with them, as sayeth the Apostle 'in the unity of the Spirit, in the bond of peace' (Eph. iv. 3), and acknowledge God's gifts in them, whether holy baptism, or the blessing of ordination, or the profession of continence, or the stability of virginity, or faith in the Trinity, and whatsoever others there may be ; yet, though they had all these, they were useless in the absence of charity. But who shall say that he possesses the charity of Christ, when he enters not into the unity of Christ ? Thus, when any such join the Church Catholic, they do not receive what they were already in possession of ; but, in order that what they formerly had may begin to be of service to them, they receive something which before was wanting to them. For in it they receive the root of charity in the bond of peace and in the society of unity, in order that those sacraments of Truth which they possess, may be held unto their deliverance and not to their damnation." *

This, remember, was written of those who had valid orders and true faith, and whose sole offence consisted in their schismatical refusal to listen to the voice of Peter.

The Anglican cause is, on many grounds, in far greater straits than was that of the Donatists ; for, whereas the orders of the latter were admitted on all hands as valid, those of the former are as universally rejected.

The Catholic Church of the West in communion with the Holy See leads the way, and ordains absolutely—as being a layman—every Anglican bishop or cleric who submits to her authority. The Greek

---

* Epistola LXI. ad Theodorum Episcopum.

Church follows her example in rejecting Anglican orders. Only lately, at the Bonn Conference, the Greek representatives, when called upon to accept such orders as valid, utterly refused ; and Dr. Overbeck, speaking for the Orthodox Greeks in his book, " Intercommunion between the English and Orthodox Churches," quotes a whole *posse* of English divines to prove that the Established Church never taught the *necessity* of Episcopal ordination ; the Roman Church, he adds, is " rigorously orthodox " in ordaining *ab initio* converted Anglicans; that "the Eastern Church can but imitate her proceedings"; and that "all further controversy is broken off and indisputably settled."* Again, he says, "The Orthodox Church does not recognize the English Church to be a Church at all."†

With both of these the Anglican Church herself is in substantial agreement. Taken, not as she exists in the hopes and wishes of the best of her children, but as a whole, concrete, and actually existing corporate body, the Established Church of England has persistently repudiated the idea that she possesses orders in our sense of the word, and is at the present moment busy in putting down those of her clergy who presume to act on any such hypothesis. So far is the necessity of Episcopal Ordination, as a divine institution, from being any part of her creed, that it was not till the passing of the Act of Uniformity in the reign of Charles II., that clergymen who officiated in the Established Church were required to have received it at all.

Those in her bosom who don the habit and office of the Catholic priest, though in her, are not of her. They can hardly conceal from themselves that they are out of humour with her whole spirit and history; they are at issue with her authority; and, if they would save themselves from being swamped by the full tide of public opinion and Ecclesiastical legislation which has set in so strongly against them, they will have to swim for their lives *against* the stream. Like Virgil's shipwrecked heroes, "Apparent rari nantes in gurgite vasto."

The *fact* that those who have busied themselves in vindicating their claim to a sacrificing priesthood have had the case decided against them by the verdict of the Christian world, is one of great significance, and ought to have much weight with persons of your way of thinking. St. Augustine, in his controversy with the Donatists, was able to appeal to this fact as being quite decisive: "*Securus judicat orbis terrarum.*" The judgment of the Christian world is against you, and that settles the question.

One of the most surprising phenomena of the present Ritualistic movement is the reliance which those who lead it place on the infallibility of the conclusions of their private judgment in this matter, such a weight of external authority to the contrary notwithstanding. So much so, that they are willing to stake the salvation of their souls on the issue; that they are in the right, and all the rest of the world is in the wrong.

Individual impressions, no matter how strong, are not infallible. Between them and external realities the gulf is great indeed, and they never can suffice to raise any opinion out of the region of the probable. The testimony of such an overwhelming number of Christians must always present an insuperable barrier to certainty, and render the theology of those who are ready to send souls into eternity on the *chance* of their being true priests quite unintelligible.

It is time now to take in hand the thesis which I propose to myself to establish to your satisfaction, viz., that to avail oneself of Anglican orders in any way must be held unlawful—for two reasons :—

I. Because historically they are doubtful.

II. Because theologically they are absolutely invalid.

I.

The historical aspect of the question is necessarily a dreary one. It would be cruelty to attempt to drag an ordinary reader through the tangle in which it is involved.

I wish rather to confine your attention to the uncertainty of those facts which are necessary to the Anglican theory, so that, even if I fail to satisfy you on the second point of my argument, I shall still leave you no escape from the conclusion. For the existence of a serious doubt, resulting from an hiatus in the chain of evidence, is quite as fatal to the lawfulness of exercising Anglican orders as their absolute invalidity. In dealing with the Sacraments, it is never lawful to follow even a probable opinion in preference to a safer one—except when the salvation of a soul is at stake, and there is no other course open. For instance, it must ever be held a sacrilege to attempt to offer the Holy Sacrifice as long as there are any serious grounds for supposing that, instead of renewing the great oblation of the new law, you may only be acting a wretched parody of the most sacred mysteries of the Christian religion.

The historical events which preclude any such certainty as could render the exercise of Anglican orders lawful are the following :—

1. The absence of any documentary evidence that Barlow ever received Episcopal consecration.

He is the father of the present Episcopacy, such as it is ; and if the case breaks down in his person, the whole succession is vitiated in its source.

Such an absence of documentary proof is only negative, and hence of itself not conclusive ; though it is a suspicious circumstance that, in the case of every other bishop where the register is missing, Professor Stubbs has been able to supply the necessary evidence of his consecration from diocesan registers, Rymer, or elsewhere.* For Barlow he has been able to do nothing. This circumstance, however, does not stand alone. The more Barlow's case is examined, the worse it appears ; and every fresh fact that comes to light goes to support the suspicion that he was never consecrated.

We know, for instance, that Henry VIII. rewarded several of his creatures with the temporalities of bishops' sees, gave them the title of bishop, and a seat in the House of Lords, and that Barlow was amongst the number. We have Barlow's opinion expressed in the plainest terms—an opinion which he held in common with the king and other Reformers—that consecration was quite unnecessary.

In addition to this, we have a copy of the restitution to Barlow of the temporalities of St. David's, lately found in the Memoranda Roll of the Remembrancer of the Lord Treasurer of the Exchequer. This form of grant is quite exceptional, and must have been drawn up to meet some special exigency. So far from being in the usual form, it is a grant of temporalities on account of the vacancy of the see, with the addition, " To hold to him and his assigns during his life " ; so that the revenues of the vacant

---

* Stubbs, " Registrum Anglicanum," page 77.

see were handed over to him for his lifetime. The writ states, moreover, that the chapter had elected Barlow for "Bishop and Pastor," and that "the Archbishop had not only confirmed him," but "preferred him to be Bishop and Pastor"; and had given, not "for the time of vacancy," not "to the said elect and confirmed," but "to the same now Bishop, for his life, all the profits in the King's hands by reason of the last vacancy of the bishopric and the custody of the temporalities."*

The omission of all mention of consecration is remarkable, as, since 1534, in consequence of Act 25 Henry VIII., cap. 20, it was usual to recite it in the writ, as well as the statement that he held the temporalities for his life, not because he held the See, which was vacant, but in virtue of the King's grant.

That this same "now Bishop" was so still only by election is evident from the writ of summons to the House of Lords issued the following day, June 12th, wherein he is described as "the Bishopp then elect of St. Asaph's, now elect of St. Davyes." Had any consecration taken place previously it must have been known to Cromwell, the King's Vicar-General, and it was from him this writ emanated.

Barlow, after this, immediately assumed the style and title of a Bishop, though up to the 12th of June he was so only by election, as is proved by the documents referred to above. To say that Barlow was spoken of and treated as a Bishop is no proof of his consecration, for he had already received what was, in the eyes of the sycophants that surrounded Henry, quite as good as consecration—the King's election, and that was sufficient. Barlow himself formulates the principle for us thus :—

* Estcourt, "Question of Anglican Ordinations," Appendix IV.

"If the King's grace, being Supreme Head of the Church of England, did chuse, denominate, and elect, any layman, being learned, to be a Bishop, that he so chosen, without mention made of any orders, should be as good a Bishop as he is or the best in England."* He was, moreover, *legally* at least, Bishop of Bath and Wells.

How little the fact of a man being styled Bishop in those days proves, we see in the case of Parker. His consecration—supposing that he was consecrated—took place 17th December. Now, we have a document, signed *per ipsam Reginam*, addressed, on the 20th of the previous October, "To the most reverend Father in Xt., Mathew, *Archbishop of Canterbury*"; and that he had the temporalities, is evident from the fact that Tunstall, who died at Lambeth, 18th November, 1559, was committed to his keeping. He was, therefore, styled Archbishop, and had possession of his See in virtue of the Queen's election some two months before his alleged consecration. These facts tell very strongly against the supposition that Barlow was a validly consecrated Bishop; in fact, that he was ever anything more than a nominee of the Crown. The amount of positive evidence to the contrary is so strong, that it is quite impossible to *prove* he was anything more than this; and until this can be done, the claim of Anglicans to an unbroken Apostolic Succession must be considered in abeyance. It does not meet the case to argue that, at all events, Hodgson was consecrated according to the rite of the Roman Pontifical; that he assisted in the consecration of Parker; and that, even if Barlow was not a Bishop, this would cover the defect. For, in the first place, it was not cer-

* Strype's "Memorials," vol. i. page 184; Records, No. 77.

tain that he was so consecrated ; and, in the second there is no sufficient authority for saying that his presence as assistant would validate a consecration in which the Consecrator was no Bishop. An assistant is present to help the principal, and, in case his act is unproductive of any result, it is simply the old story over again of John helping Tom. " What are you doing, John ?" " Helping Tom, sir." " What are you doing, Tom ?" " Nothing, sir."

2. The next historical fact of importance bearing on the case is that Barlow, his associates, and successors, were heretics. They held and taught false doctrine, and on no point were they more at issue with the ancient Church of England than on the nature and office of the Christian priesthood. This I need not stay to prove, for you and all who think with you hold such men convicted of heresy.

It is only necessary to take up any High Church publication to find their modern representatives,— the Barings, the Jacksons, and Bickersteths of the day,—held up to public reprobation as ignorant heretics. This is another shadow cast over the claim of Anglicans to a certainly valid priesthood. Orders conferred by heretics have, in certain cases, not been received by the Church. Though there is, I admit, a strong case in favour of their validity, there is also a strong case against them (Bingham, Antiq., iv. 7). And the existence of this strong case against them is fatal to their claim being recognized as certainly substantiated, until, at least, the Church has pronounced in their favour. Without this guarantee heretical ordinations cannot be regarded as *safe.* You will recollect the distinction made between the orders of the Miletians and those of the Novatians and Donatists as bearing upon this point.

3. The third important fact in the list is the
omission of the tradition of the instruments. This
portion of the ceremony is, it is true, not primitive;
still it was part of the existing rite at the time,
used to render more explicit the declaration of the
nature of the office conferred, and cannot be omitted
without prejudice to the *status* of those so ordained.
Benedict XIV.* mentions the case of a priest, who
by accident omitted to receive the instruments from
the Bishop. On the case being brought before the
Sacred Congregation, it was decided that he must
be ordained again *conditionally.* What, then, is to
be said of the intentional omission of this part of
the Ordination Service, coupled as it was with
the omission of everything that had been considered
of the essence of the priesthood? If the former
omission was sufficient to render ordination probably invalid, the latter very much increases the
probability.

4. The uncertainty as to valid baptism leaves
the whole question of Ordination in inextricable
confusion. The denial of baptismal regeneration
has from the beginning been a tradition found in
the Anglican Church. By the Gorham Judgment it
has been given a legal recognition, and has been
declared an opinion which any clergyman may
hold and act upon. This opinion had always been
acted upon by a certain number, whose lax practice rendered valid baptism almost impossible. We
are all familiar with the old-fashioned cleric, who
baptized with a damp finger, or who did not use
water in winter, as it was too cold for the babies,
or who, standing on one side of the font, sprinkled
a few drops of water at sundry bundles of clothes
held by several women on the other. All these

* Syn. Dioc., viii. 10.

practices combined to rear up generations of men who could neither confer nor receive valid orders.

Mr. Bennett, of Frome, bears witness to the fact, without apparently perceiving how deeply it affects the question of his orders. In an article on "Some Results of the Tractarian Movement," published amongst "Essays on the Church and the World,"* edited by Orbly Shipley, he says, "Strange; yet not more strange than true, that Baptism as a Sacrament was well-nigh lost amongst the English people. Common basins were brought into the churches; while the fonts were made into flower-pots for the garden of the parsonage. It is very questionable whether water, when used, really did touch the person of the child meant to be baptized. The prayers which in the Baptismal Office asserted the doctrine of a new birth, were frequently altered in the recitation, or altogether omitted. The water was not blessed or consecrated, and the whole service was studiously mutilated to escape the doctrine which it involved."

Dr. Newman also bears witness to the fact, and estimates its bearing on the question of Orders as follows :—" Previous baptism is the condition of the valid administration of the other Sacraments. When I was in the Anglican Church I saw enough of the lax administration of baptism, even among High Churchmen, though they did not, of course, intend it, to fill me with great uneasiness. Of course there are definite persons, whom one might point out, whose baptisms are sure to be valid. But my argument has nothing to do with *present* baptisms. Bishops were baptized not lately, but as children. The present bishops were consecrated by other bishops; they, again, by others. What I

* Page 9, 1867.

C

have seen in the Anglican Church makes it very
difficult for me to deny that every now and then a
bishop was a consecrator who had never been baptized.   Some bishops have been brought up in the
North as Presbyterians, others as Dissenters, others
as Low Churchmen, others have been baptized in
the careless, perfunctory way so common ; there is,
then, much reason to believe that some consecra-
tors were not bishops, for the simple reason that,
formally speaking, they were not Christians.   But,
at least, there is a great presumption that, where
evidently our Lord has not left a rigid rule of baptism, He has not left a valid ordination." *

That Baptism as a Sacrament was well-nigh lost
amongst the English people up to the time of the
Tractarian movement renders it quite impossible
to trace out a certainly valid Apostolic Succession.

5. It is beyond dispute that the founders of the
Anglican Church held Episcopacy to be a lawful
and praiseworthy form of Church government, but
they were very resolute against the idea that it was
of divine institution, or was able to confer grace,
or was a sacrament.   This is abundantly proved
both by the words and the acts of the Reformers.
Tyndale pronounces on the question of the ministry
as follows :—" We choose temporal officers and read
their duty to them, and they promise to be faithful
ministers, and then are admitted.   Neither is there
any other manner of ceremony at all required in
making of our spiritual officers than to choose an
able person, and then to rehearse him his duty and
give him his charge, and so to put him in his
room."†

Jewel follows in the same strain :—" How are
we to speak of the ministry of the Church, which

---

* The *Month*, September, 1868, page 271.
† " Obedience of a Christian Man," vol. i. page 259, ed.
Parker Society.

some have called Holy Orders? Shall we account
it a Sacrament? There is no reason to do so. It
is a heavenly office, a holy ministry or service. By
such as have this office God lighteneth our darkness,
He declareth His mind to us, He gathereth together
His scattered sheep, and publisheth to the world
the glad tidings of salvation. The Patriarchs did
bear this office. This was the office of the Prophets.
. . . No doubt the ministering of the Gospel is highly
to be esteemed, seeing our Saviour was not ashamed
to publish the will of His Father in His own person;
yet it appeareth not wherever He did ordain it to
be a Sacrament".*

On this subject Bishop Cooper's language is
remarkably clear and strong. He maintains, in
his "Answer to Martin Marprelate," printed in
1589, "that no form of Church government is
divinely ordained; that Protestant communities,
in establishing different forms, have only made a
legitimate use of their Christian liberty; and that
Episcopacy is peculiarly suited to England, because
the English Constitution is monarchical" (Macaulay's "History of England," vol. i. p. 77, ed. 1862).

Cranmer has not hid his light under a bushel.
His answer to certain questions on the Sacraments
are given by Collier (vol. ii. Appendix 49) :—" Q.
11. Whether a Bishop hath authority to make a
priest by the Scripture or no? And whether any
other but only a Bishop may make a priest? A. 'A
Bishop may make a priest by the Scripture, and so
may Princes and Governors also, and that by the
authority of God committed to them, and the people
also by election.' And in the next answer he says,
'In the New Testament he that is appointed to be
a bishop or a priest needeth no consecration, by the

* "A Treatise of the Sacraments," Works, vol. ii.
page 1129.

c 2

Scripture; for election or appointing thereto i sufficient.'"

It was only to be expected that men with such views should act up to them. Accordingly, we have an instrument by which Archbishop Grindal, Primate of All England in 1582, authorizes John Morrison, a Scotch minister, ordained by the General Synod of County Lothian of the Reformed Church of Scotland, to preach and administer the Sacraments in any part of the province of Canterbury.

In the year 1603, the Convocation (Canon 55) declared the Church of Scotland to be a true part of the Holy Catholic Church of Christ; and in it there is no Episcopal ordination or control. To meet this view also, the expression ordination by "imposition of hands" was corrupted into ordination "by election" in the Protestant Bibles of 1562, 1577, and 1579.

In fact, it was not till the passing of the Act of Uniformity in 1662, more than a hundred years after the Reformation began, that Episcopal ordination was made a condition for holding office in the Established Church.

"It was by the Act of Uniformity, passed after the Restoration, that persons not Episcopally ordained were, for the first time, made incapable of holding benefices.

"No man was more zealous for this law than Clarendon. Yet he says, 'This was new; for there had been many, and at present there were some, who possessed benefices with cure of souls, and other Ecclesiastical promotions, who had never received orders but in France or Holland; and these men must now receive new ordination, which had always been held unlawful in the Church, or by this Act of Parliament be deprived of their livelihood, which they enjoyed in the most flourishing and peaceable time of the Church'" (Macaulay "History of England," vol. i. p. 79). The same author states, that as many as two thousand such ministers resigned in one day rather than take orders by ordination from a Bishop.

Not only, then, are Anglican orders untrustworthy, because for nearly three hundred years there was no certain baptism, but also because for over a hundred there can be no certainty about ordination.

Some time ago there was a movement for bringing about an interchange of communion between the Anglicans and the Swedes. Dr. Pusey argued, with much force, against any such attempt, on the ground that where there was no valid priesthood there could be no true Bishops, and that the Swedish forms were insufficient to make a priest. Dr. Littledale followed him in the same line of argument. If this be true—as it most certainly is in the case of the Swedes—what becomes of the Anglicans during the period preceding the Act of Uniformity?

Here, then, are five facts of history, as hard and dry as you could wish. The total result is that they leave the whole question in such a tangle of uncertainty that it is quite hopeless to attempt to unravel it by the aid of history alone. Any one of them is enough to cast a doubt on the validity of Anglican orders—enough to render any attempt at using them, in a Catholic sense, unlawful. All of them taken together render it almost an impossibility that they could be valid.

It is quite a mystery to me that a man like Dr. Forbes, who must have known these things, could make such a statement as this : " It is *absolutely certain* that Anglican orders are valid and regular, unless the Pope's recognition be essential " ("On the

Thirty-nine Articles," vol. ix. p. 717). He ought to have said rather, "unless it be quite clear that *certainly* valid Episcopal ordination, *certainly* valid priesthood, *certainly* valid baptism, true doctrine and tradition of the instruments be essential." The absence of any of these things we know to be fatal to absolute certainty.

To assume that Barlow, because he acted as bishop, *must* have been consecrated, and then to busy oneself about fixing the date at which his consecration *must* have taken place, is not the way in which impartial critics handle evidence upon whose correct estimation issues of grave moment depend.

II.

So far we have dealt only with the historical side of the question ; we have confined ourselves to the consideration of facts which it is impossible to deny, and of their bearing on the lawfulness of exercising Anglican orders in view of the doubts which these facts raise as to the possibility of an unbroken succession.

Here theology comes in to our assistance ; it throws fresh light on the subject, and enables us to take a step forward. Historical doubts may suffice to prove the unlawfulness of exercising Anglican orders without closing the question of their validity. It has been by the light of theology, and not of history, that the Church has been able to decide, without any hesitation, that they are not only doubtful, but absolutely invalid.

Holding her theological principles in her hand, like so many threads of Ariadne, she has been enabled to wind her way through the labyrinth of difficulties which bewilder a student who approaches the question without any such guidance.

To the consideration, therefore, of these theological principles we must now direct our attention.

A Sacrament is defined by the Book of Common Prayer to be " an outward and visible sign of an inward and spiritual grace given unto us, ordained by Christ himself, as a means whereby we receive the same, and a pledge to assure us thereof."

This definition is sufficient for our purpose, for it mentions (1), the outward visible sign ; (2), inward spiritual grace; (3), institution by Jesus Christ ; and these are what are generally considered essential to the nature of a Sacrament.

The outward visible sign is composed of two parts ; (1), the Matter—the visible thing done or used, whose nature as a Sacrament is determined by the form ; (2), the Form—that part of the Sacrament which sanctifies the matter, so as to bestow on it the power of causing grace, and which, ordinarily at least, consists in the words pronounced by the minister.

If it is asked why any particular form of words has power to sanctify the external matter in such a way that it not only contains grace itself, but also has the power of causing grace to exist in the souls of those to whom it is applied, the only answer to such a question is, because Christ has selected them for that purpose.

In the same way, the only reason why the external visible cause, bread, produces the inward effect, life ; and why other things—wood, for instance—do not, is that God has created the former for the purpose, and the latter He has not so created.

Hence it has always been a first principle in theology, that any one who does not use the form instituted by Christ, either directly or indirectly, or substantially alters it, cannot possibly confer

the Sacrament that results from the application of
the external matter which that form was ordained
to bless and consecrate.

It is, moreover, necessary that the person who
uses the outward and visible sign does so for the
purpose of conferring the Sacrament; else the result
in the spiritual world is *nil.* For instance, it may
often fall to the lot of an elderly priest to instruct
the younger clergy in the manner of conferring
the sacraments, and. although the whole rite may
be gone through with the utmost accuracy, no
sacrament is conferred, because what was done was
not done *for the purpose* of conferring the Sacrament, but for some other.

Keeping these principles steadily in view, we are
now in a position to approach the question of the
validity of the Anglican rite of Consecration.

Up to the time of the Reformation the rite of
Consecration of Bishops was made up of the imposition of hands, accompanied by certain prayers, one
or other of which was doubtless the form of the
Sacrament. Now, the Church has not as yet decided what exact part constitutes the form ; hence
the necessity for not expunging any important part
is all the greater, lest in doing so we omit something
essential.

"In truth, the Catholic rite, whether it differs
from itself or not in different ages, still in every
age, age after age, is itself, and nothing but itself.
It is a concrete whole, one and indivisible, and acts
per modum unius ; and having been established
by the Church, and being in possession, it cannot
be cut up into bits, be docked and twisted, or split
into essentials and non-essentials, genus and species,
matter and form, at the heretical will of a Cranmer
or a Ridley, or turned into a fancy Ordinal by a
Royal commission of divines, without a sacrilege

perilous to its vitality" (Newman's "Essays,
Critical and Historical," vol. ii. p. 82).

If the Church ever does interfere with the rite
for conferring the Sacraments, it is chiefly by way
of addition; she distinctly disclaims all right to
make any substantial alteration. (Council of Trent,
Sess. 21.)

In estimating the nature of the change in
the mode of consecrating, the Reformers have
saved us a great deal of trouble by the cleanness
with which they did their work. They were no
clumsy bunglers; but men of decided views. They
proposed to themselves to give practical expression
to their views on orders in the ritual, and they did so.

In the Anglican Ritual devised by Cranmer in
the reign of Edward VI., the following equivocal
and meagre exhortation was substituted for the form
in the Pontifical:—"Take the Holy Ghost; and
remember thou stir up the grace of God which is in
thee by the imposition of hands; for God hath not
given us the spirit of fear, but of power and love
and soberness."

These words are accompanied by imposition of
hands, and are hence the only ones that can claim
to be the Form of the Sacrament. They are quite
ambiguous; they do not determine the action any
way, for they mention neither the order to be conferred nor the special end for which the words are
used.

They are, moreover, of recent origin. The latter
portion is an innovation of Cranmer and Co.; the
former, "Take the Holy Ghost," may be taken as a
substitute for the words "Receive the Holy Ghost,"
&c., used in the third imposition of hands in the
old Ritual, which, however, was not introduced into
it till about the fourteenth century, as Martine has
proved ("De Antiquis Ecclesiæ Ritibus").*

* Lib. I. art. x. n. 14.

The whole of that part of the service by which,
and by which essentially, orders had been conferred
in the West for the first fourteen centuries was swept
clean away ; all that was left was an addition,
made to render the rite more explicit, and claiming
no higher antiquity than the 14th century. Whatever part of the Ritual, therefore, may claim to be
the form instituted by Jesus Christ for giving the
grace of Orders, this clearly cannot put forward
any such claim. For, in order to take up such a
position, it would be necessary to adopt the suicidal
defence, either that the form of the Sacrament has
been altered, which would mean that the Sacrament had been destroyed—for the matter and form
have always been considered of the essence of the
Sacrament—or that the ancient Church had no
true priesthood or legitimate ministers. Courayer,
whom Anglican writers have championed so lustily,
sees the force of this argument so plainly that
he maintains that the words, " Receive the Holy
Ghost" cannot be the form of the Sacrament, for
reasons which he takes from Morinus.*

It is curious that he and his following do not
see that thereby they cut from under their feet
the only defence on which the validity of Anglican
orders could stand.

Dr. Lingard also perceives this difficulty, and
sees no alternative but to accept the monition
tacked on to the words : " Take the Holy Ghost,"
as the only portion of the service that could be
regarded as a substitute for the " Prayer of Consecration " in the old Rituals, which was generally
considered to contain the essential Form of Holy
Orders. He deals with the question as follows :—

" However, setting Barlow aside, there still re-
mained the very important question, whether the

* " Dissertation," page 111.

Lambeth rite was of itself sufficient to constitute a
Christian bishop; for the reader is not to suppose
that the consecration of Dr. Parker was celebrated
according to the form in which Episcopal consecrations are performed at the present time. In
Edward's reign Archbishop Cranmer had 'devised
an ordinal, in conformity with his own Calvinistic
notions respecting the Episcopal character. It
seems, however, not to have harmonized perfectly
with the notions which Barlow and his coadjutors
had acquired from their foreign masters. Omit-
ting, therefore, part of it, they consecrated the new
Archbishop in the following manner. Placing
their hands upon his head, they admonished him
thus:—'Remember that thou stir up the grace of
God which is in thee by imposition of hands, for
God hath not given us the spirit of fear, but of
power and love and of soberness.' How, it was
asked, could this monition make a bishop? It
bore no immediate connection with the Episcopal
character. It designated none of the peculiar
duties incumbent on a bishop. It was as fit a
form for the ordination of a parish clerk as for the
spiritual ruler of a diocese. Parliament, in the
eighth of Elizabeth, ordered that the ordinal devised under Edward VI. should be observed, which
ordinal continued in force till the Convocation in
1662 made the following alteration in the form to
be henceforth observed : — 'Receive the Holy
Ghost *for the office and work of a bishop in the
Church of God, committed unto thee by the imposition of our hands in the name of the Father and of
the Son and of the Holy Ghost ;* and remember that
thou stir up the grace of God which *is given to
thee by this imposition of our hands ;* for God hath
not given us the spirit of fear, but of power and
love and soberness.' This addition was mani-

festly a great improvement, inasmuch as it imparted to the rite that Episcopal character which it had hitherto wanted ; but, to have been of any real use, it ought to have been introduced at the same time with the line of prelates to whom it applied. By Charles II. it was approved, and at his recommendation was established by Parliament as the legal form of ordaining bishops in the Church of England. Statutes of Realm, V." ("History of England," vol. vi. Note C.)

We must also bear in mind that the new Anglican Ritual was drawn up to suit the new doctrine, which was a direct contradiction of the teaching of the old Church of England on the nature of the Sacrament.

Our forefathers had been simple enough to believe that Orders was a sacrament, which, like all sacraments, conferred grace, as a superadded and abiding quality on the soul, and impressed a *character* which constituted the priesthood. The new teachers changed all this, and held that Orders was not a sacrament ; that it was only an appointment to an office ; that the mode of appointment was not a divine institution, and had no promise of grace attached to it ; that they were, in fact, ministers, whose chief office was that of public speaking and public reading.

Here, then, we have to deal, not simply with an accidental omission, nor with an omission which had no doctrinal significance in the eyes of those who were responsible for it, but with a change made by those who had no right to make it, and made for the purpose of putting an end for ever to all claim to the inheritance of Orders as a sacramental grace on the part of those so ordained. The teaching of the 25th Article is quite clear on the point, where it says that Orders is one of those things "not to be counted for Sacraments of the Gospel, being such as have grown partly of the corrupt following of the Apostles, partly are states of life allowed in the Scriptures ; but yet have not the nature of Sacraments with Baptism and the Lord's Supper, for that they have not any visible sign or ceremony ordained of God."

Hence, even if what was said or done might otherwise have been in itself sufficient, the fact that the words used were not used as a sacramental form, and that the alteration made in them was made with a view of excluding all question of grace, and of preventing their being considered any part of a sacramental sign, is sufficient to hinder any bestowal of grace.

It is not said, or even implied, that a man who holds an heretical opinion on the nature of a Sacrament may not confer it validly, provided the form and intention of the Church have not been interfered with. When, however, as in this case, the heretical view annihilates the very essence of the Sacrament, and is given external expression by corrupting the essential prayers or ceremonies— for the matter and form of the Sacraments, as Benedict XIV. teaches in his work, " De Synodo Deæcesana" (l. viii. c. 10), belong to the substance of the Sacrament, and are declared by the Council of Trent to be unalterable (Sess. 21, c. 2).—it must be held to vitiate the whole proceeding. Such must be the judgment of theology, according to the principle of St. Thomas Aquinas :— " He who corrupts the sacramental words in uttering them, if he does this on purpose, does not appear to intend that which the Church does, and thus the Sacrament does not appear to be perfected" (P. 3, q. lx., a. 7, ad. 3). It must be borne in mind that St. Thomas, in writing his Summa, does not profess

to do more than furnish a summary, for the use of
students, of those principles of theology which had
been handed down to his times by the unbroken
tradition of what some are pleased to call the
undivided Church.

It may, then, be accepted as proved :—

1. That in the Ordinal of Edward VI., those
parts which had up to that time been held to constitute the Sacramental forms, indispensable to the
validity of the Sacrament, by which—and up to
the 14th century, by which alone — Episcopal
Orders were conferred, were omitted bodily.

2. That in the consecration of Parker even the
Ritual of Edward VI. was not followed.

3. That these alterations were made to give
expression in the rite to the view that Orders were
not a visible sign or ceremony ordained of God,
had not the nature of a Sacrament, and bestowed
no grace. (Compare Art. 25 with the definition of
a Sacrament in the Catechism given previously.)

" Dr. Champneys and all Catholics," says
Clerophilus Alethes,* " have ever attacked their
Orders from the defect of that form." It may be
well, therefore, to produce some evidence of the
fact, and to see what effect this denial had upon
both Catholics and Protestants in their dealings
with Anglican Orders. For this purpose it will be
necessary to enter, at some length, upon the history
of the period. The light which it throws upon
the subject will reward us for our labour.

Very soon after the alleged consecration of
Parker, the Catholic party openly challenged the
valid ordination of those of the new learning, and
called upon them to produce, if they could, evidence
of the fact.

The following are a few specimens of their line
of argument :—

* Page 237.

1. Harding fastens upon Jewel, and takes him to task in this wise:—" Ye have abandoned the external Sacrifice and Priesthood of the New Testament, and have not in your sect consecrated Bishops, and therefore, being without Priests made with lawful laying on of hands, as Scripture requireth, all Orders being given by Bishops only, how can you say that any among you can lawfully minister, or that you have any lawful ministers at all?"

He compares Jewel to Ischyras, who was no lawful minister, as he was not lawfully ordained, because Collythus, who pretended to ordain him, " died in the degree of Priesthood himself, and was never consecrated Bishop " (Harding's " Conference of Jewel," p. 58).

He concludes his argument as follows :—" Thus they be neither Priests nor Deacons which be not lawfully consecrated according to the order that is used in the Church, that is, to wit, by Bishops lawfully consecrated, but either by the people as the lay magistrate . . . or by monks and friars apostate, or by excommunicated Priests having no bishoply power."

Again, he pursues Jewel in these words :—" You, Jewel, bear yourself as though you were Bishop of Salisbury. But how can you prove your vocation ? By what authority usurp you the administration of doctrine and the Sacraments? What can you allege for the right and proof of your ministry ? Who hath called you ? Who hath laid hands on you ? By what example hath he done it? How and by whom are you consecrated ? Who hath sent you ? Who hath committed to you the office you take upon you? Be you a priest or be you not ? If you be not, how dare you usurp the name and office of a Bishop ? If you be, tell us who gave you orders ? The institution of a Priest was

never yet but in power of a Bishop. . . . Show
us the letter of your Orders. At least show us
that you have received powers to the office you
presume to exercise, by due order of laying on of
hands and consecration. But order and consecration you have not. . . . Though the Prince
has thus promoted you, yet ye be presumers and
thrusters in of yourselves. Well, lands and manors
the Prince may give you ; Priesthood and Bishopric
the Prince cannot give you." To all this, all that
Jewel could answer was that he was bishop by
" election," and that Harding was one of those
who elected him.

Dr. Stapleton also follows Harding's line of
argument, thus :—" Now the *pretended* Bishops of
Protestantism—whereas the whole number of our
learned and reverend Pastors, for confession of the
truth, were displaced of their rooms, none being
left in the realm having authority to consecrate
Bishops or make Priests, that being the office of
only Bishops—by what authority do they govern
the fold of Christ's flock ? Who laid hands upon
them ? . . . Whither went they to be consecrated—into France, Spain, or Germany—seeing
that at home there was no number of such as
might and would serve their turn ? . . . I say,
therefore, by the verdict of Holy Scripture and
practice of the primitive Church, these men are no
Bishops. I speak nothing of the laws of the
realm : it hath been of late sufficiently proved they
are no Bishops, if they be tried thereby. But let them
be tried by Scripture. . . . Your pretended
Bishops have no such ordination (as the ancient
Bishops had), no such laying on of hands of other
Bishops, no authority to make true Priests or
Ministers, and, therefore, neither are ye true
Ministers, neither are they any Bishops at all "
(" Fortress of the Faith," p. 36).

The same writer, when dealing with Jewel's "Untruths," says, that these men had "rushed into the ministry without any imposition of hands, and without any ecclesiastical authority"; and at page 93, that they "began from themselves, receiving imposition of hands from nobody."

This writer's "Return of Untruths," his challenge to Jewel and Horn, and his Counterblast against them, are worth your perusal.

Bristow wrote some nine years later than Harding or Stapleton. He was Professor of Theology both at Douay and at Rheims, and deals with the question as a professed theologian. He calls the new ministers "laymen, unsent, uncalled, unconsecrated" ("Motives," p. 91, 1574). "The King of England," he says, "and the Queen too, give their diplomas to whom they choose. Then these carry themselves as Bishops, and begin to ordain ministers."

"We have," he says again, "many examples in England—to wit, in the case of Parker, Grindal, Saunders, Horne, and others—who, having been ordained Priests according to the Catholic rite, were judged fit to be, without any ordination, not only Priests, but also Bishops, Archbishops, and Primates, either by virtue of royal letters, or by a ridiculous consecration by those who had received the power of consecrating only from the Queen" (p. 264—266).

This repeated assertion that Anglican orders had no higher sanction in their origin than the royal authority, tends much to strengthen the suspicion that Barlow was Bishop only by royal "election"; a title which, we have seen, he held to be both sufficient and legitimate. For it would have been ruin to their cause if these writers grounded their charge on statements of fact which they did not know to be true, and which the parties most concerned could easily prove to be false.

The Council of Trent had its attention directed to the question by Pope Pius, and were considering the expediency of condemning Anglican orders by a formal decree. They were prevented from doing so only by the intervention of the Spanish Ambassador, who opposed the expediency of issuing such a decree on two grounds : first, that it was unnecessary ; because it was perfectly notorious that Anglican Prelates were no Bishops ; and secondly, because such a proceeding would most likely irritate the English Government. "All the world knows," he says, " that Anglican Bishops are impostors ; but, if you exasperate the English Government, you will only make the condition of English Catholics still more intolerable than it is at present."

On the death of Edward VI., and the accession of his sister Mary, the *status* of the newly-ordained clergy was a question that received her immediate attention. The claim to possess valid orders was a pretence of such notoriety that she deals with it as a fact beyond dispute, on which it was not necessary to wait for the Church to adjudicate. In her letter to Bonner, Art. 15, she directs :—" Item, touching such persons as were heretofore promoted to any orders, after the new sort and fashion of orders, considering they were not ordered in very deed, the Bishop of the diocese, finding otherwise sufficiency and ability in these men, may supply that thing which wanted in them before, and then, according to his discretion, admit them to minister."

Now the thing that was wanting in them was that they were not " ordered in very deed."

The Bishops, made after the new sort and fashion of orders, were deprived of their sees for various

reasons. The Commissions for proceeding against
them are dated in March, 1553-4, and are given in
Rymer (xv. 70). Taylor, of Lincoln, was deprived
expressly "on account of the *nullity* of his consecration and defect in his title, which he held from
King Edward VI. by letters-patent, with this
clause : 'during his good behaviour.'" ("Canterbury Register," March 20.) Hooper, who had
been consecrated by the Revised Ritual, was deprived on the same day for the same reason. Farrer, of whom Collier says that his consecration
"had not been altogether performed after the old
form,"* was also deprived on the same day, for the
same reason. Harley was deprived with him, on
the same grounds. Bird and Holgate, for their
marriage. Bush resigned. Scory had to give up
Chichester to the lawful bishop, Day, and on his
repentance was allowed to act as Priest. It is
also a fact worthy of being remembered, that when
some of these "pretended" Bishops were degraded,
before they were handed over to the secular power
they were treated simply as Priests, and degraded
only from the Priesthood, no notice being taken of
their consecrations according to the Revised Ritual.
Latimer, Farrer, and Ridley were dealt with in
this way.

When Pole landed in England in the following
November, there were, therefore, no Bishops, after
the new sort and fashion of orders, in the possession
of any see, left for him to deal with. It is sufficiently probable that the English authorities were
in communication with the Pope, and acted with
his knowledge and sanction. The fact that their
acts were not in any way questioned or appealed
against, on the arrival of Pole, seems to point to

* Part II. book iv. no. 266.

that conclusion. However, we have no ceitain information on the point.

The work of the legate in England lay chiefly amongst the lower order of clergy. Some of them had been validly ordained according to the Roman Ritual, under Henry VIII., others had been ordained with cuts and omissions to suit the fancy of the Reformers. Others had been ordained in accordance with the the new Ritual, and some not at all. In addition to this, heresy, schism, simony, and incontinence had brought upon some or other of them nearly every censure and punishment known to the canon law. It was, therefore, necessary that every case should be judged on its own merits, and that Cardinal Pole should not only have very large powers himself, but be able to delegate these powers to others, as it was quite impossible for one man to deal with every case likely to arise in consequence of the late state of affairs. Accordingly, Cardinal Pole received from Pope Julius III. a Bull, dated March 8, 1554, authorizing him to subdelegate to others the very large legatine faculties he had already received.

The perusal of this document is very instructive, as it shows how thoroughly the situation was understood at Rome. Speaking of those clergy who by reason of their crimes had incurred the censure of irregularity, he says that on repentance they may be absolved and allowed to exercise their orders— "provided," however, "that before their fall into this heresy they had been rightly and lawfully promoted or ordained."

This clause excludes those who had been ordained by the Edwardine forms, for they had been ordained and promoted in direct violation of the canon law, and therefore unlawfully. We shall find later on that the evil thing about their ordination and appointment was, that it was not done according to the form and intention of the Church.

Another passage deals more directly with the question before us, as it separates off the ecclesiastics in England by the condition of the Orders they laid claim to.

The Pope empowers the legate "Freely to use all and each of the aforesaid . . . . faculties . . . . in person, or through others appointed by thee for this purpose *pro tem.*, even as regards orders which they had never or evilly received, and the rite of Consecration which was applied to them by other bishops or archbishops, even heretics and schismatics, or otherwise unduly and without following the accustomed form of the Church."

Here we have mention of three classes of persons to be dealt with : (1) Those who had not received orders ; (2) Those who had received them evilly ; (3) Those who had received them unduly.

Under which of these classes, then, are the Edwardine clerics to be ranked? We have seen that Queen Mary, acting certainly under advice, ranks them in the first category by the words : "Seeing they are not ordered in very deed." As do also the Bishops, who deprived Taylor, with other Edwardine prelates, expressly on the ground of the "nullity of his consecration."

Now, is there any reason to suppose that Cardinal Pole differed from the Queen and the Catholic Bishops in his estimate of the Revised Ordinal? Quite the contrary. Not only did he allow their decision to hold good, but also, in the Commission granted to the Dean and Chapter of Canterbury for reconciling the clergy and laity of that Province, he expresses this agreement.

"The instrument," says Collier, "extends to the absolving of all persons who repent their miscarriages, and desire to be restored from all heresies, schisms, apostasies, from all excommunications, suspensions, and other ecclesiastical censures ; and more particularly the clergy who had received orders from any schismatical or heretical bishops, officiated in virtue of that character, and complied with any unallowed ceremonies and forms of prayer are absolved, *provided the Form and Intention of the Church was not omitted in their ordination.*"*

I have shown already, beyond all question, that this was the very thing done in the Revised Ritual. Both the Form and the Intention of the Church were tampered with. Schismatical and heretical orders are allowed to stand after repentance and absolution ; not so, however, in the case where the Form and Intention of the Church were omitted.

You will notice that the two points insisted on throughout these quotations are—(1) Unlawfulness of title or promotion ; (2) Invalidity of Orders, in the case of those promoted after the new sort and fashion of orders.

On the death of Queen Mary, her sister, Queen Elizabeth, set herself to undo the work of the last reign, and to introduce again the new religion, and, along with it, the Revised Ordinal. The difficulties in her way were serious. None of the Bishops of the English Hierarchy would have anything to do with her or her Ordinal. They were, therefore, deposed, with the exception of Kitchen, of Llandaff. As they refused to hand on the succession to the Queen's nominees, and as they were the only persons who could lawfully do so, on the principle, " *Quod non habetis, non potestis dare,*" the lawful succession in the Church of England would on their death become extinct. In this extremity, the Queen

* Part II. book v. no. 377.

bethought herself of her Royal Supremacy in spiritual matters over the Church, and on her own authority commissioned four of her creatures to consecrate Parker by an instrument in which the following dispensation was inserted, to cover all the irregularity and deficiency in the proceeding :— " Supplying, nevertheless, by our supreme Royal authority, of our mere motion and certain knowledge, if anything either in those things which shall be done by you according to our foresaid mandate or in you or any one of you is or shall be wanting in condition, *status*, or faculty, of those things which are required or are necessary by the statutes of this kingdom or by Ecclesiastical laws in this matter, the nature of the time and the necessity of the circumstances requiring it."

This clause is remarkable from the use of the technical terms " of our mere motion and certain knowledge," which are used in Papal documents to indicate their unreserved application to all cases.

Those who confirmed Parker in his dignity quote this clause in their commission as the authority for their acts. They say, " The election of the venerable man, Mr. Mathew Parker, we confirm by the supreme authority of the said most serene Lady, our Queen, committed unto us in his behalf ; supplying by the supreme royal authority, of the Queen's mere motion and certain knowledge, delegated to us, all defects in this election, as well in those things done by us and proceeded with according to the commandment given us, or that are or shall be in ourselves or in the condition, *status*, or capacity of any one of us for this performance " (Bramhall, iii. 202). Nor is this all.

The validity of the consecration of Parker and also the validity of the consecrations of the Queen's bishops, as well as their lawful authority, were seriously questioned in many quarters, and doubts were freely expressed on the subject. To set the whole matter at rest, an Act was passed in 1565 (8 Eliz. c. l.), to decree " that all acts and things heretofore had, made, or done by any person or persons in or about any *consecration,* confirmation, or investing of any person or persons elected to the office or dignity of any Archbishop or Bishop within this realm, or within any other the Queen's Majesty's dominions or countries, by virtue of the Queen's Majesty's letters patent or commission since the beginning of her Majesty's reign, be and shall be *by the authority of this present Parliament* declared, judged, and deemed, at and from every of the several times of the doing thereof, good and perfect to all respects and purposes ; *any matter or thing that can or may be objected to the contrary thereof in any wise notwithstanding.*"

If it be within the scope of the civil power to make good and perfect consecrations in holy orders by the authority of Parliament—anything to the contrary notwithstanding — then those of the Queen's bishops are, beyond question, valid. You, however, agree with me so far, that the Apostolic succession and valid orders must have a higher sanction than even the weighty authority of the British Parliament.

The Catholics were not the only persons who pronounced the Revised Ordinal worthless. The Scotch Presbyterians, on the very same grounds, argued that there were no Bishops in the Establishment ; that, in fact, it was Presbyterian because the Ordinal was insufficient to make a Bishop. So straight did they drive their argument home, that in order to meet it the Consecration Service was altered to its present form—a hundred years and more too late to be of any use to the line of prelates which it introduced.

Burnet, in his " History of the Reformation," *
speaks of this alteration as follows :—" They agreed
on a form of ordaining deacons, priests, and bishops
which is the same we yet (*i. e.* A.D. 1683) use,
except in some few words that have been added
since in the ordination of a Priest or Bishop. For
there was then no express mention made, in the
words of ordaining them, that it was for the one
or the other office. In both it was said, ' Receive,
thou the Holy Ghost, in the name of the Father,
&c.. . . . But that having been since made use of to
prove both functions the same, it was of late years
altered as it is now."

Such then, in short, are the considerations which
ought to guide an inquirer as to the validity of
Anglican Orders, and which seem to me sufficient,
for all practical purposes, to close the question. I
have confined my remarks, as you cannot fail to
have noticed, chiefly to the consecration of Bishops,
because, if there are no validly consecrated Bishops
there can be no orders of any kind in the Established Church.

I have maintained, from an historical point of
view, the *unlawfulness* of attempting to exercise
such Orders, (1), Because of the grave reasons there
are for thinking that some at least of the Protestant
Bishops were never formally even Christians, on
account of their never having received any certainly
valid Christian Baptism, and hence were incapable
of receiving any valid Christian Orders. That there
have been some such is beyond a doubt ; and the
very loose theology and practice of former days on
the subject of baptismal regeneration render it more
than probable that there have been many others.—
(2) Because we know for certain that, till the

* Part II. book i. page 144, ed. 1683.

Act of Uniformity was passed, a very large number of persons acting as clergy never even pretended to have received ordination to the priesthood from any Bishop. These grave doubts as to Baptism and Priesthood create a state of uncertainty as to the existence of Orders in any given case, in which it is not safe, and hence not *lawful*, to act.

I have further maintained the absolute *invalidity* of Anglican Orders because of the omission in the Revised Ritual, amongst other things, of the " Prayer of Consecration," which had, up to that time, been considered part of the essential sacramental Form of Holy Orders. An omission made without any authority, and one so serious, that you might almost as well hold that if the words, " I baptize thee in the name of the Father," &c. were omitted in baptism, the other passages in the Ritual would supply the deficiency.

The only answer that can be attempted to this is, to say that our Lord ordained His Apostles by the form, " Receive the Holy Ghost," and that the Holy See in the case of the Abyssinian ordinations has allowed the sufficiency of this Form.

But, in the first place, you know that theologians generally hold that Christ determined, substantially at least, the Matter and Form of all the Sacraments before His Ascension, and the fact that the words, " Receive the Holy Ghost," were not used in the West till about the 14th century, would seem to leave no question as to their not being the Sacramental Form ; for, if so, this sacrament has been lost to the Church.,

The power of the Priesthood is twofold : one, sacramental, over the real Body of Christ in the Holy Eucharist. This power was given to the Apostles by the words : *"Do this in commemoration of Me."* And hence the Council of Florence, in

the Decree of Union, has laid down that "The
Form of the Priesthood is this : '*Receive power to
offer sacrifice for the living and the dead, in the name
of the Father,*'" &c., which is substantially the same
as the former. Without the bestowal of this power
Orders are impossible. The other power of the
Priesthood is judicial *in foro interiore* over the mys-
tical body of Christ. This is the power that is considered to be given by the words, "Receive the
Holy Ghost," and can be given only to one who is
already a Priest. Our Lord Himself conferred
them separately, as is evident ; giving the former
at the Last Supper, and the latter after the Resur-
rection. The *sine quâ non* of the Priesthood, *i.e.*
power to consecrate, was not given on the lattter
occasion by the words then used.

As regards the decision of the Holy See in refe-
rence to Abyssinian Orders, you are probably by
this time aware that Canon Estcourt, who put forth
the opinion you allude to, laboured under a very
serious misapprehension. He was quite wrong in
supposing that therein the sufficiency of the words,
"Receive the Holy Ghost," as a Sacramental Form,
was established. Even if it were so for the Priesthood, nothing would follow as regards the Episcopacy. However, I submit for your perusal the
repudiation by the Holy See of any intention to
decide the matter in this sense.

*Letter of Cardinal Patrizi to his Eminence the
Cardinal Archbishop of Westminster.*

"To the Lord Cardinal, Archbishop of Westminster.—April 30, 1875.

"Most Eminent and most Reverend Lord,—In
your letter of the 24th of August of last year, your
Eminence called attention to a question now dis-

cussed by several writers as to the meaning attach-
ing to a certain 'decree,' as it is termed, issued by
the Supreme Congregation of the Holy Inquisition
on the 10th of April, 1704, in a certain Abyssinian
case, regarding the validity of ordination conferred
by the words, " *Receive ye the Holy Ghost*,' joined
with imposition of hands; and (you mentioned)
that it had given the Anglicans ground for asserting
and boasting that in future Catholics could enter-
tain no doubt of the validity of Anglican Orders.
Wherefore, to remove all cause of anxiety and to
defend the truth more securely, your Eminence
requested a solution of the following doubt: namely,
whether the doctrine that imposition of hands joined
to these words only, ' *Receive ye the Holy Ghost*,'
suffices for the validity of the Order of Priesthood,
was contained implicitly or explicitly in the above-
named decree.

" On Wednesday, the 24th of the present month,
it was decided by the Most Eminent Fathers the
Cardinals, who share with me the office of Inquisitor
General, after a mature discussion of the question,
that an answer must be returned *in the negative*.
And one or two of the motives which guided them
in this decision will suffice to convince your Eminence of the justice of this Decree. For it is
manifest from the Coptic rite, as given in their
Pontifical books, that the words, ' *Receive ye the
Holy Ghost*,' do not constitute the entire form;
nor is the meaning of the document dating from
1704 (which document is not a Decree of the Sacred
Congregation, as appears from its Archives) to be
understood as implying more than this—that the
ordination of a Priest among the Copts, conferred
by the laying on of hands and the pronouncing of
the form prescribed by their ancient rite, is to be
considered valid; nor has the Holy Supreme Con-

gregation ever declared, explicitly or implicitly,
that the imposition of hands with no other words
than ' *Receive ye the Holy Ghost* ' suffices for the
validity of the Order of Priesthood.

" With the consciousness of having complied with
the duties of my office, it only remains for me to
kiss, with all due reverence and humility, your
Eminence's hand.

> "Your Eminence's most humble and
> devoted servant,
> "(Signed)   C. CARDINAL PATRIZI.

"Rome, April 30th, 1875."

Some persons who seem to forget that discretion
is the better part of valour, may perhaps resent
what I have written as an attack upon their
honour and an insult to their Church. With such
I do not care to dispute ; you know me too well
to suppose for a moment that I have any such intention.

I have written solely with the view of bringing
home to you what I believe to be the truth, and in
the spirit of the most perfect charity. This is a
question upon which the salvation of your soul
may depend, and eternity is altogether too serious
an issue to allow of your risking it at a game of
rouge et noir; for this is what you are doing now.

The whole Catholic Church never has accepted
and never can accept Anglican Orders, and never
ceases to cry aloud to those who would sustain the
spirits of their followers by asserting that when they
come over in a body she will make terms with them,
" No illusions, gentlemen—no illusions ! "

On the other hand, what have you to fall back
upon ? Beyond the assurance of your leaders and
your own private judgment—nothing. What guarantee have you that both they and you may not

be mistaken ? None whatever. Suppose you find, when it is too late, that you have made a mistake —what then ? The whole of the Catholic Church, the Schismatical Greek Church, even the body you called your Mother Church, were witnesses to you that you were clinging to a phantom. You would not have it so ; you staked your soul on the issue that you were right and all the world in the wrong —and you have lost.

Yours sincerely,

J. D. BREEN.

THE END.

Wyman & Sons, Printers, Great Queen Street, London, W.C.

www.ingramcontent.com/pod-product-compliance
Lightning Source LLC
Chambersburg PA
CBHW031812090426
42739CB00008B/1251